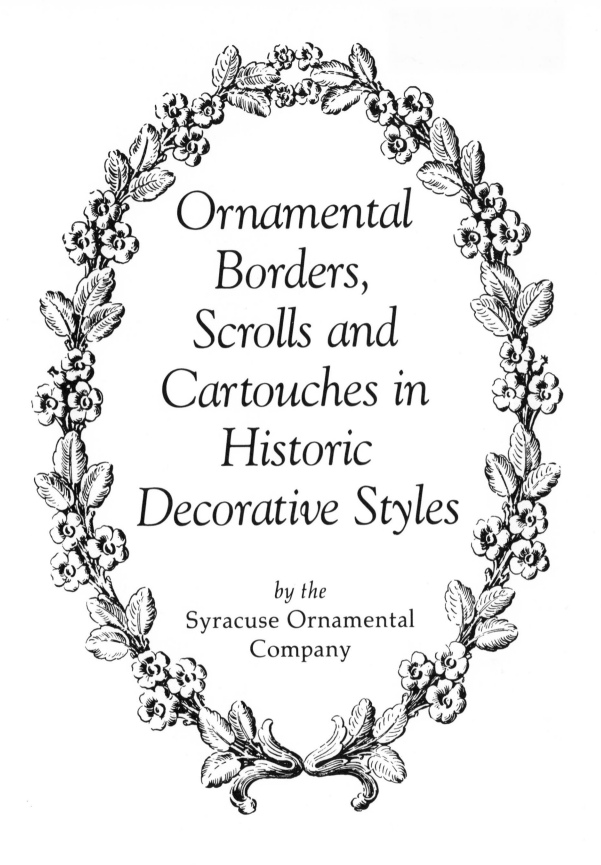

# Ornamental Borders, Scrolls and Cartouches in Historic Decorative Styles

by the
Syracuse Ornamental
Company

DOVER PUBLICATIONS, INC.
NEW YORK

# Publisher's Note

In 1923 the Syracuse Ornamental Company of Syracuse, New York advertised its fiber-wood carvings, moldings and furniture trimmings in an elegantly illustrated 432-plate catalog. It contained thousands of beautifully rendered pen-and-ink drawings, the bulk of which depicted an extensive and varied array of period furniture ornamentation. The period styles represented ranged chronologically from antiquity to the late nineteenth century, and included Grecian, Byzantine, Gothic, Renaissance, Louis XIV, William and Mary, Queen Anne, Georgian, Louis XV, Chippendale, Colonial, Louis XVI, Adam, Hepplewhite, Sheraton, Duncan Phyfe, Chinese and Modern motifs. The present edition, a new compilation of those plates from the now-rare original catalog that offer the most outstanding selection of border, scroll and cartouche elements, contains examples of each of these styles. Even though the designs were originally created strictly for the purpose of complementing pieces of furniture, contemporary artists, designers and craftspeople will find these reproductions of them ideal for any number of graphic uses. There are over 1,950 ornaments in all.

Borders are the dominant element on Plates 1–15, scrolls (including decorative "spots" and other compact elements) on Plates 16–84, and cartouches on Plates 85–126. In many cases, you'll find more than one kind of ornament on a particular page, often including a diverse assortment of vignettelike decorative devices. Within each elemental division, the plates are arranged roughly in chronological order by period style. Captions identify the dominant element and the style for each plate, when possible. The plates on which the style is not identified (either because the various styles of the designs on that plate are too numerous to enumerate or because the designs on that plate are essentially "styleless" simplified or generic variations) follow those plates of like elements on which the style is identified.

Published in Canada by General Publishing Company, Ltd., 30 Lesmill Road, Don Mills, Toronto, Ontario.

Published in the United Kingdom by Constable and Company, Ltd., 10 Orange Street, London WC2H 7EG.

*Ornamental Borders, Scrolls and Cartouches in Historic Decorative Styles* is a new selection of 126 plates from the work originally published as "Catalogue 'K'" by the Syracuse Ornamental Company, Syracuse, New York, in 1923 under the title *Period Carvings: A Catalogue Containing One-half Size Reproductions of Original Designs Done in Pen and Ink and Representing an Elaborate Selection of Carvings and Moldings of Rare Execution and True to the Periods.* The selected plates have been reordered in the present edition. The textual and pictorial matter that appeared in the margins of the original plates has been deleted, as have the catalog numbers and cross-sections of moldings within the plate areas. The Publisher's Note and the captions have been prepared specially for this edition. The specific style identifications are taken verbatim from the original plates.

### DOVER *Pictorial Archive* SERIES

Manufactured in the United States of America
Dover Publications, Inc., 31 East 2nd Street, Mineola, N.Y. 11501

**Library of Congress Cataloging-in-Publication Data**

Period carvings. Selections.
Ornamental borders, scrolls, and cartouches in historic decorative styles.

(Dover pictorial archive series)
Reprint. Originally published: Period carvings. Syracuse, N.Y. : Syracuse Ornamental Company, c1923.
1. Wood-carving—Catalogs. 2. Woodwork—Catalogs. I. Syracuse Ornamental Company. II. Title. III. Series.
NK4799.P4725 1987     745.4          87-22148
ISBN 0-486-25489-5 (pbk.)

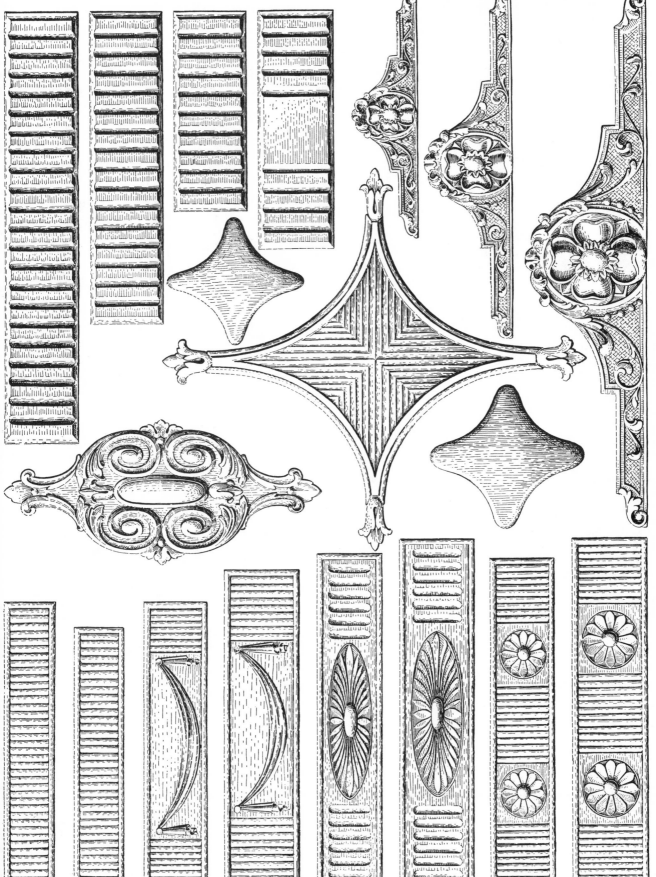

*Plate 1*   Borders: Adam and Hepplewhite

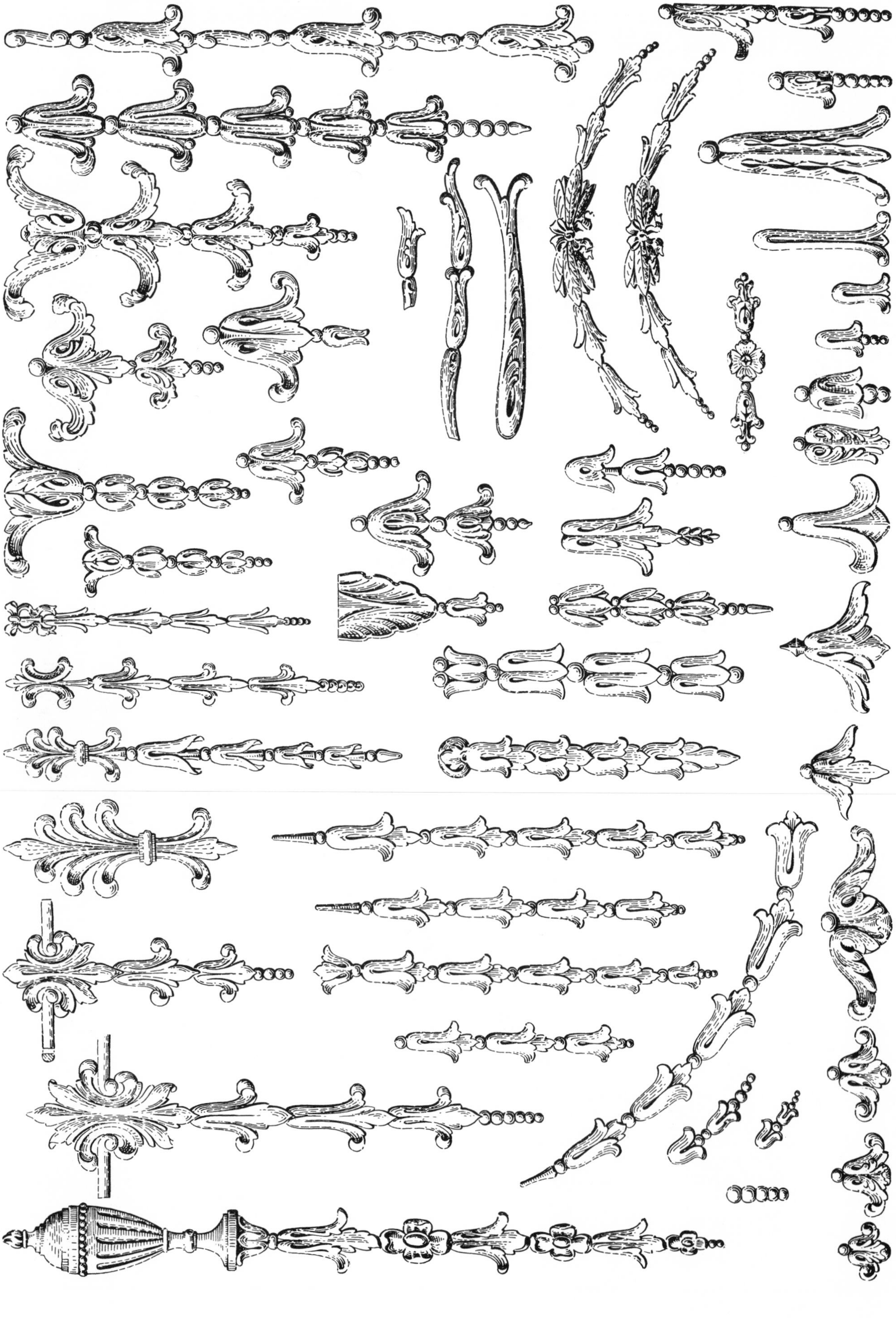

*Plate* 2 Borders: Adam and Hepplewhite

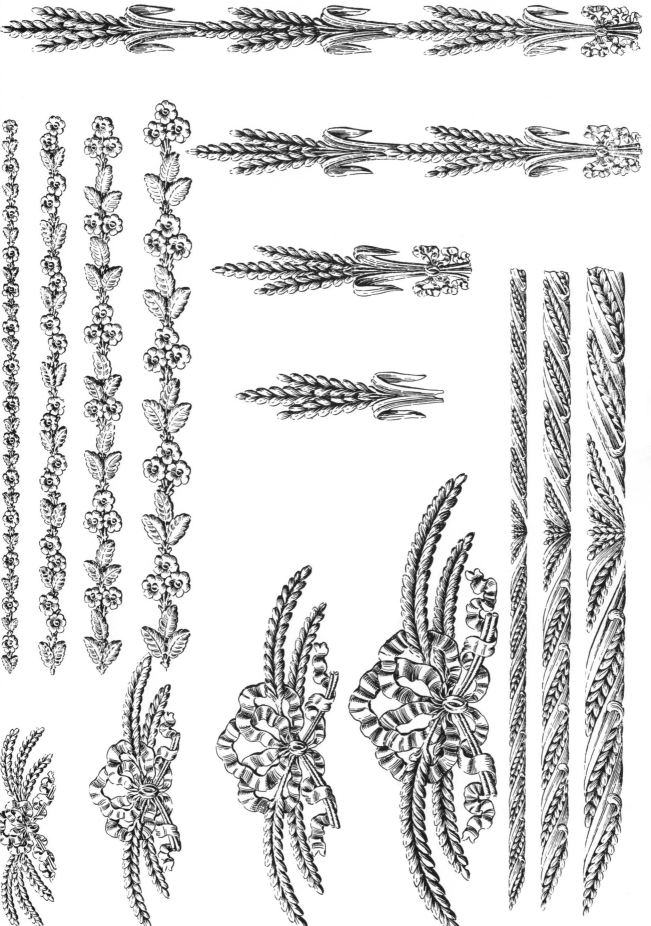

*Plate 3*   Borders: Hepplewhite

*Plate 4* Borders: Modern Style

*Plate 5*   Borders: Modern Style

*Plate 6* Borders: Various Styles

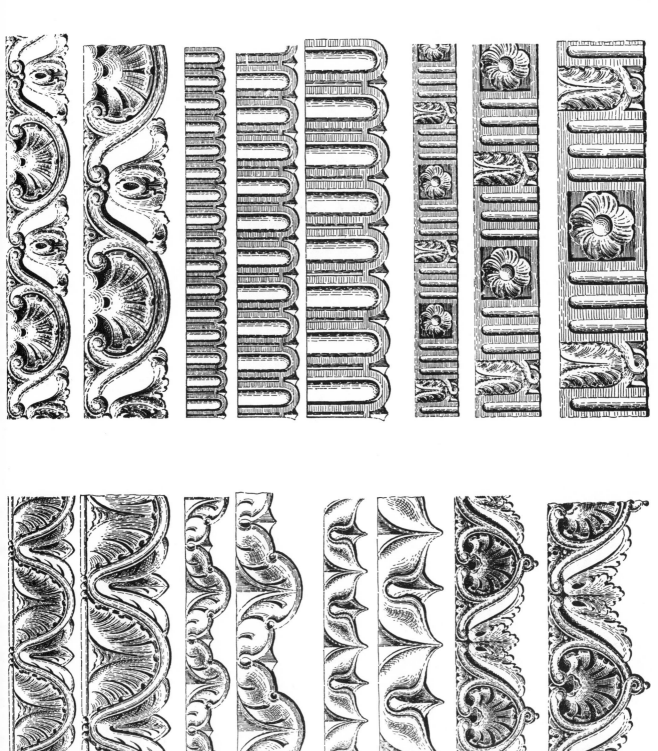

*Plate 7*  Borders: Various Styles

*Plate 8* Borders: Various Styles

*Plate 9*  Borders: Various Styles

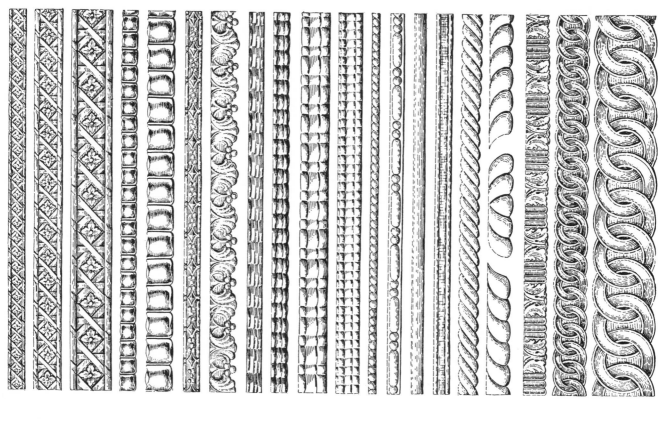

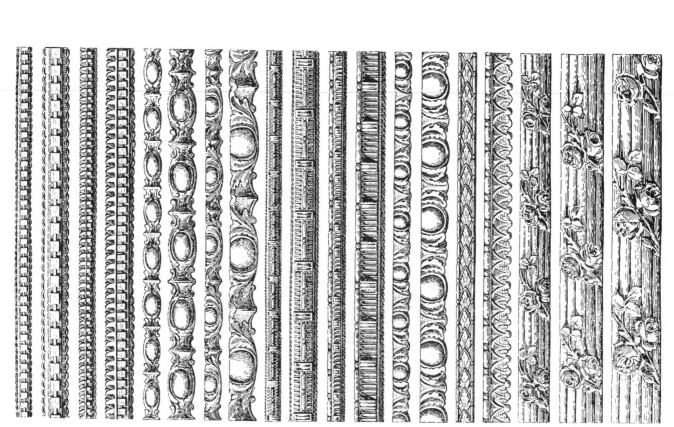

*Plate 10* Borders: Various Styles

*Plate 11*   Borders: Various Styles

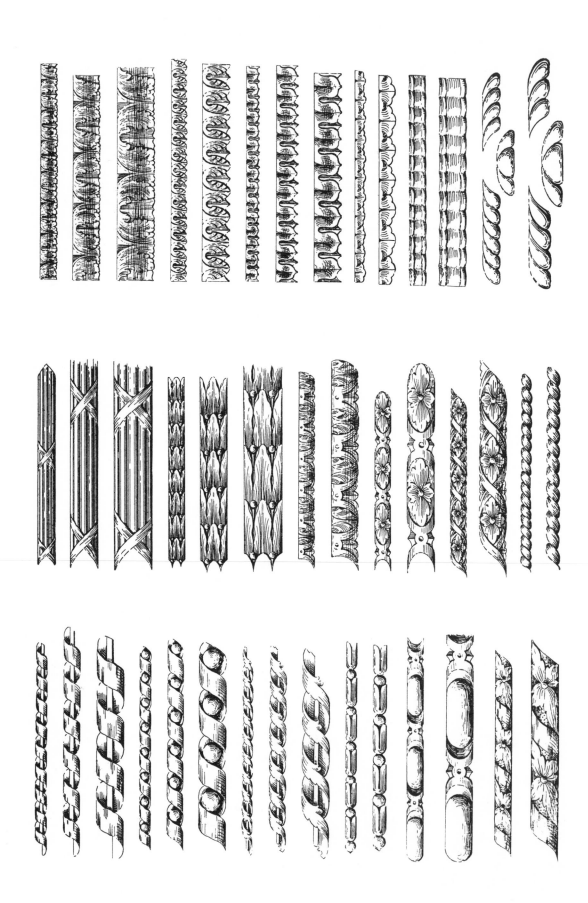

*Plate 12* Borders: Various Styles

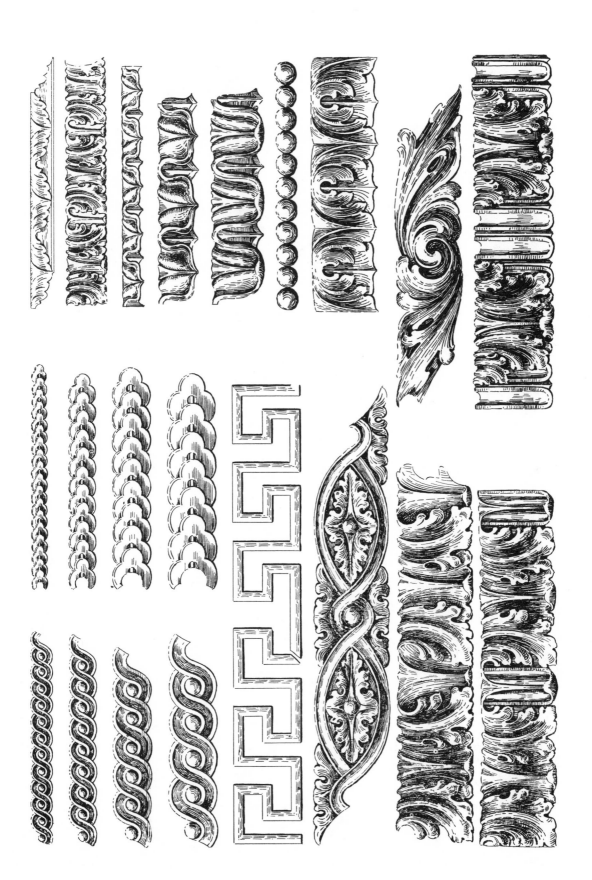

*Plate 13* Borders: Various Styles

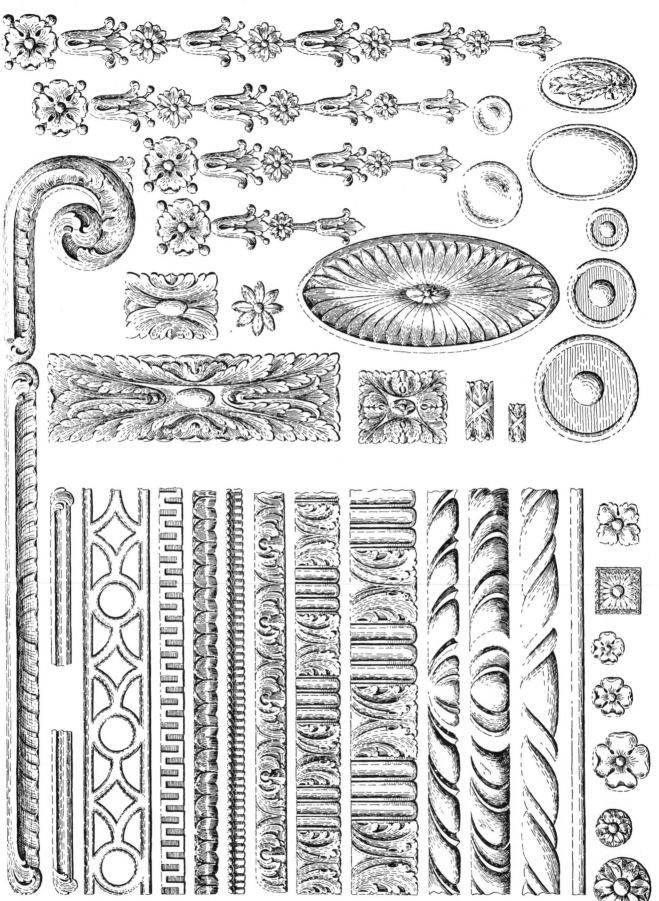

*Plate 14* Borders: Various Styles

*Plate 15* Borders: Various Styles

*Plate 16   Scrolls: Grecian Motif*

Plate 17   Scrolls: Byzantine (Modern Adaptation)

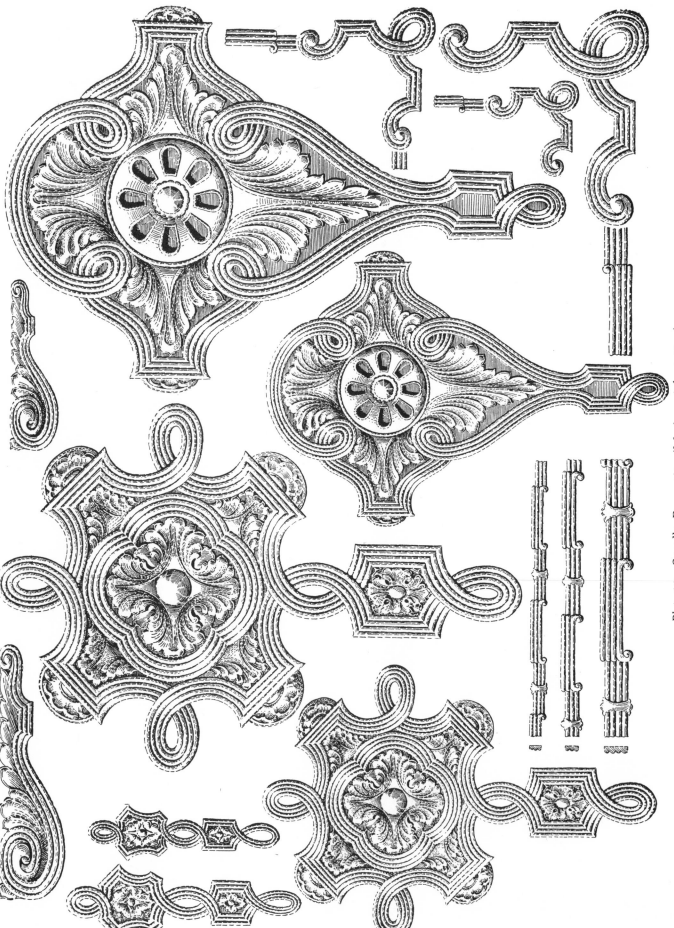

Plate 18 Scrolls: Byzantine (Modern Adaptation)

Plate 19    Scrolls: Renaissance

*Plate 20* Scrolls: Renaissance

Plate 21 Scrolls: Renaissance

Plate 22   Scrolls: Renaissance

Plate 23   Scrolls: Renaissance

Plate 24   Scrolls: Renaissance

Plate 25  Scrolls: Renaissance

Plate 26    Scrolls: Renaissance

Plate 27 Scrolls: Renaissance

Plate 28   Scrolls: Renaissance

*Plate 29* Scrolls: Renaissance

Plate 30   Scrolls: Renaissance

Plate 31  Scrolls: Renaissance

Plate 32  Scrolls: Renaissance

*Plate 33* Scrolls: Renaissance

*Plate 34* Scrolls: English Renaissance

*Plate 35   Scrolls: English Renaissance*

Plate 36   Scrolls: English Renaissance

Plate 37   Scrolls: Louis XIV

Plate 38   Scrolls: Louis XIV

Plate 39 Scrolls: Louis XIV

Plate 40  Scrolls: Louis XIV

*Plate 41* Scrolls: Queen Anne and William and Mary

Plate 42   Scrolls: Queen Anne and William and Mary

*Plate 43* Scrolls: Queen Anne and William and Mary

*Plate 44*  Scrolls: Queen Anne and William and Mary

Plate 45   Scrolls:  Queen Anne and William and Mary

*Plate 46* Scrolls: Queen Anne and William and Mary

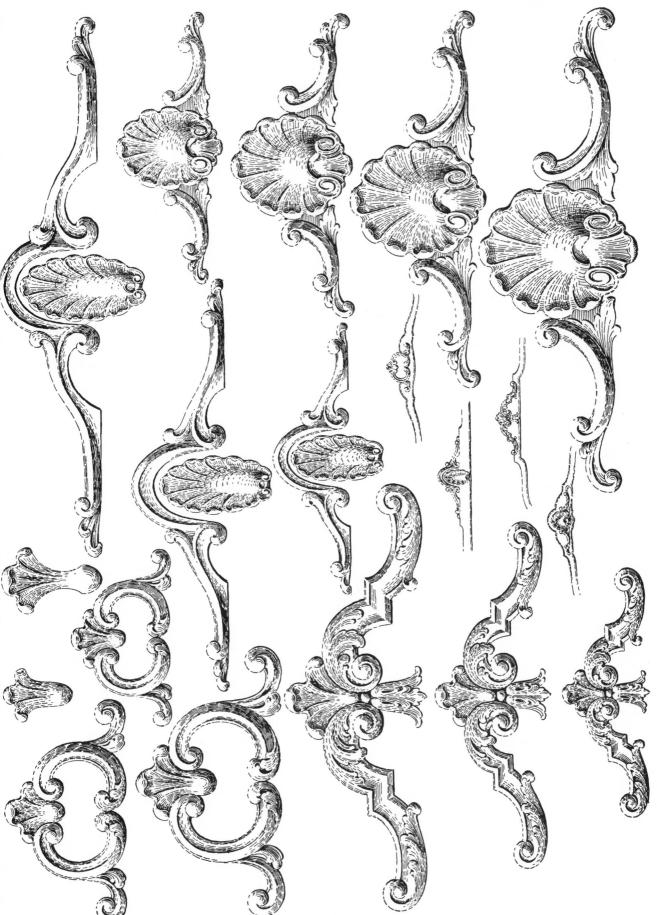

*Plate 47* Scrolls: Queen Anne and William and Mary

*Plate 48   Scrolls: Queen Anne, William and Mary and Chippendale*

Plate 49   Scrolls: Queen Anne

Plate 50   Scrolls: Queen Anne

Plate 51  Scrolls: Queen Anne

Plate 52    Scrolls: Queen Anne

Plate 53   Scrolls: Queen Anne

*Plate* 54 Scrolls: Georgian and Louis XIV

*Plate 55   Scrolls: Georgian and Louis XIV*

Plate 56    Scrolls: Georgian and Louis XIV

*Plate 57* Scrolls: Georgian

Plate 58  Scrolls: Georgian

Plate 59    Scrolls: Georgian

*Plate 60* Scrolls: Georgian and Chippendale

*Plate 61*   Scrolls: Georgian and Chippendale

*Plate 62* Scrolls: Louis XV

*Plate 63* Scrolls: Louis XV

Plate 64   Scrolls: Louis XV

Plate 65   Scrolls: Georgian Chippendale

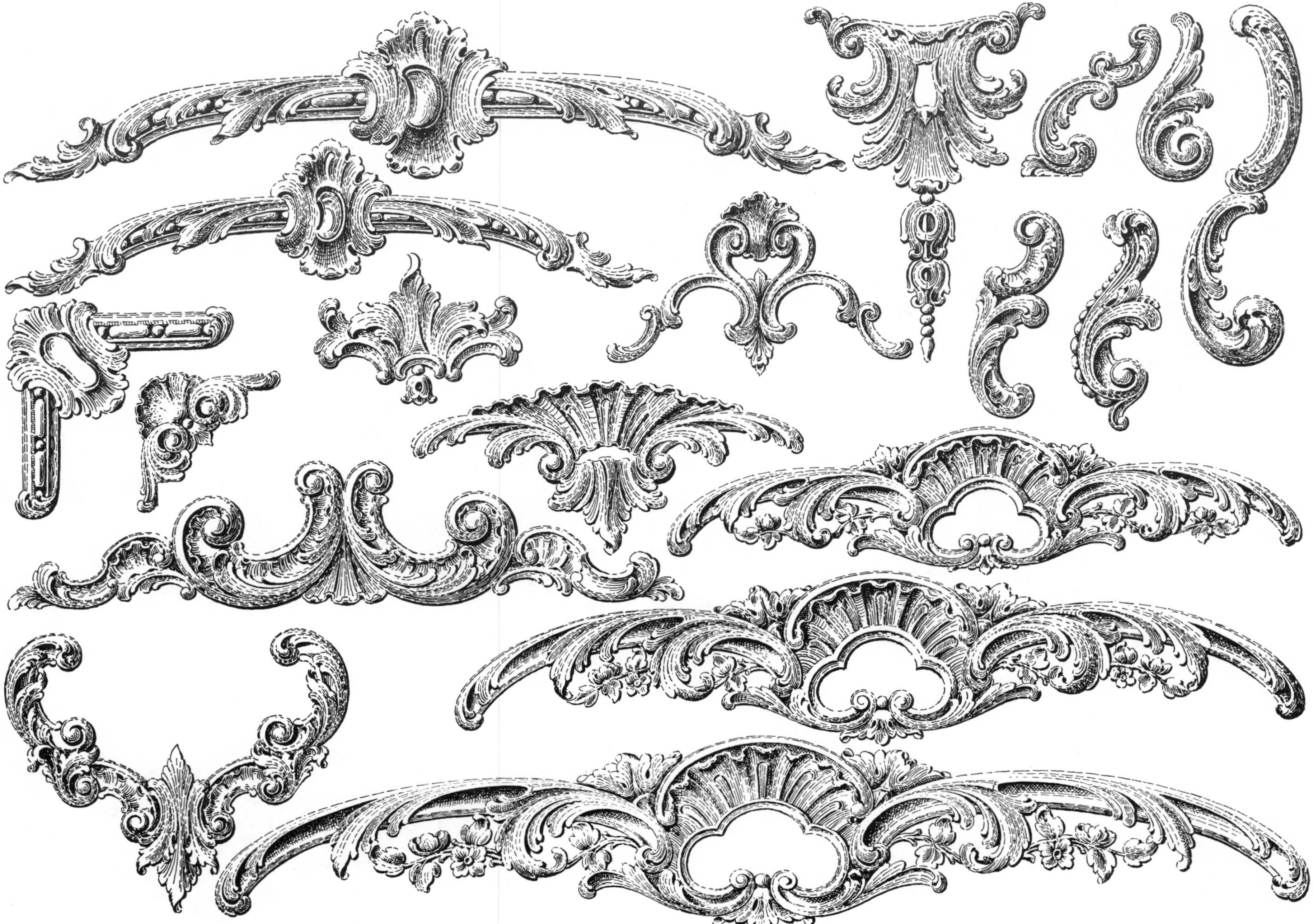

*Plate 66* Scrolls: Chippendale

*Plate 67*  Scrolls: Chippendale (French and Chinese)

Plate 68    Scrolls: Chippendale (French and Chinese)

Plate 69   Scrolls: Chippendale (French and Chinese)

Plate 70   Scrolls: Chippendale (French and Chinese)

Plate 71   Scrolls: Colonial

Plate 72   Scrolls: Colonial

Plate 73   Scrolls: Louis XVI

Plate 74   Scrolls: Louis XVI

Plate 75　Scrolls: Louis XVI

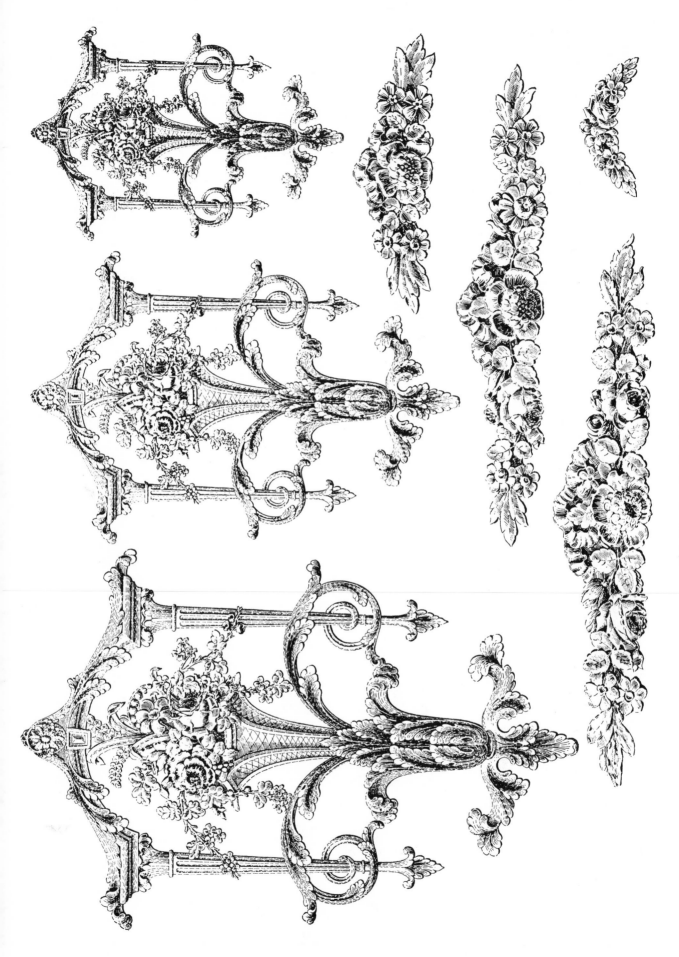

*Plate 76   Scrolls: Louis XVI*

Plate 77   Scrolls: Hepplewhite

*Plate 78   Scrolls: Hepplewhite*

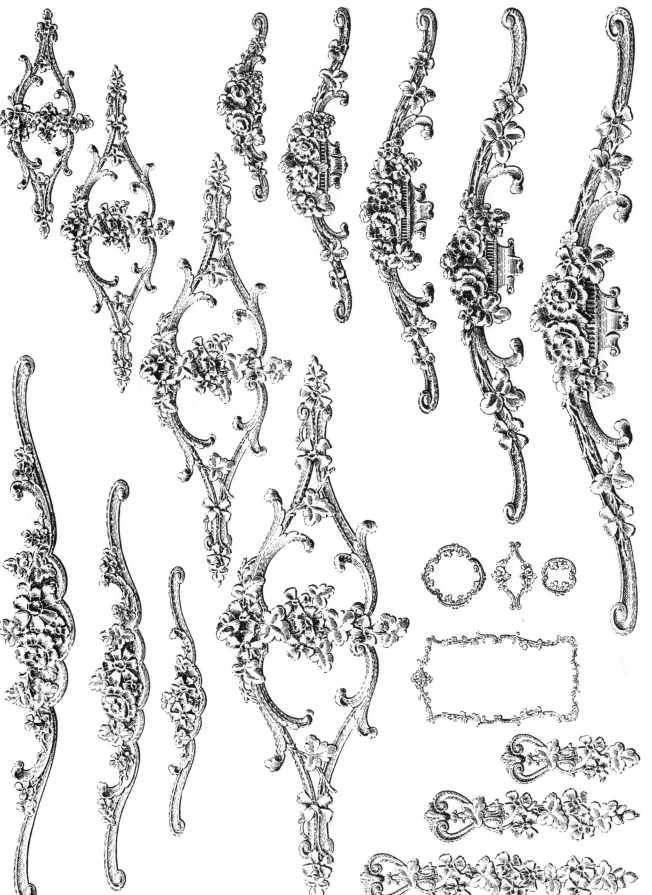

Plate 79   Scrolls: Sheraton and Louis XVI (Modern Adaptation)

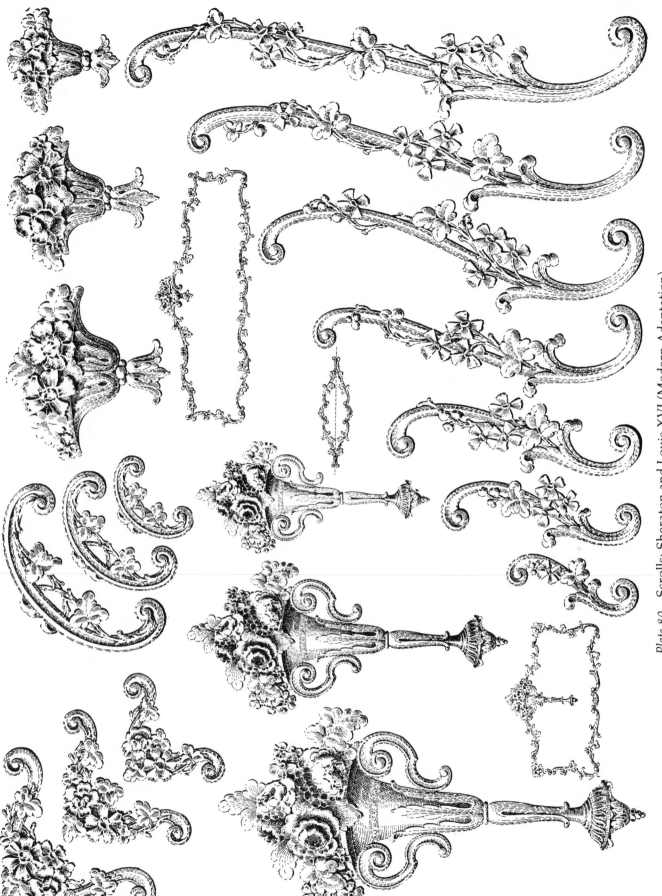

Plate 80   Scrolls: Sheraton and Louis XVI (Modern Adaptation)

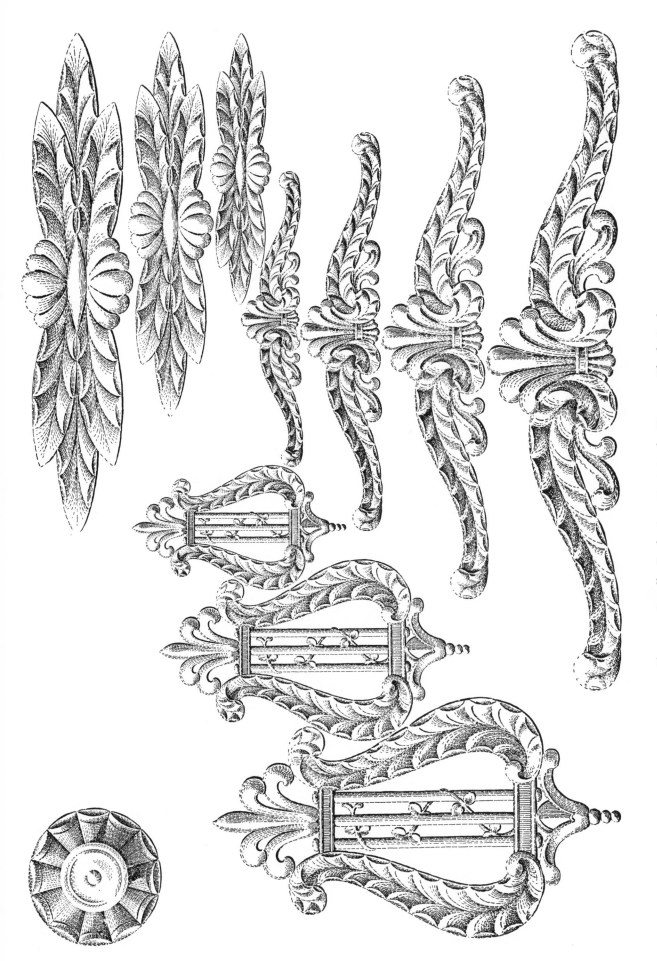

*Plate 81*   Scrolls: Early American in the Duncan Phyfe Style

Plate 82   Scrolls: Generic Variations

*Plate 83*  Scrolls: Generic Variations

Plate 84   Scrolls: Generic Variations

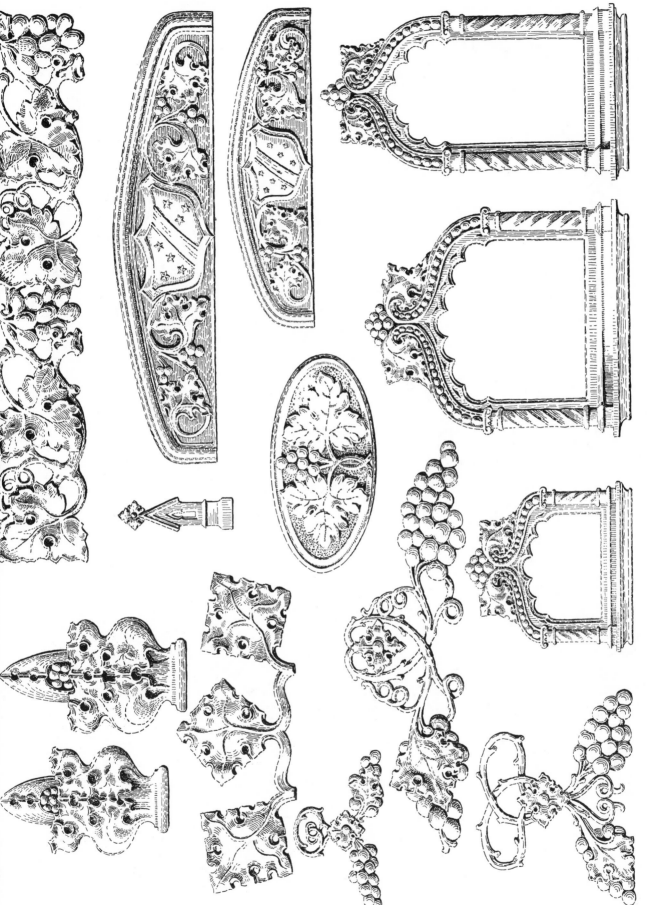

*Plate 85* Cartouches: Gothic

Plate 86  Cartouches: Renaissance

*Plate 87* Cartouches: Renaissance

*Plate 88* Cartouches: Renaissance

Plate 89  Cartouches: Renaissance

*Plate 90* Cartouches: Renaissance

Plate 91 Cartouches: Renaissance

*Plate 92* Cartouches: Louis XIV and Chippendale

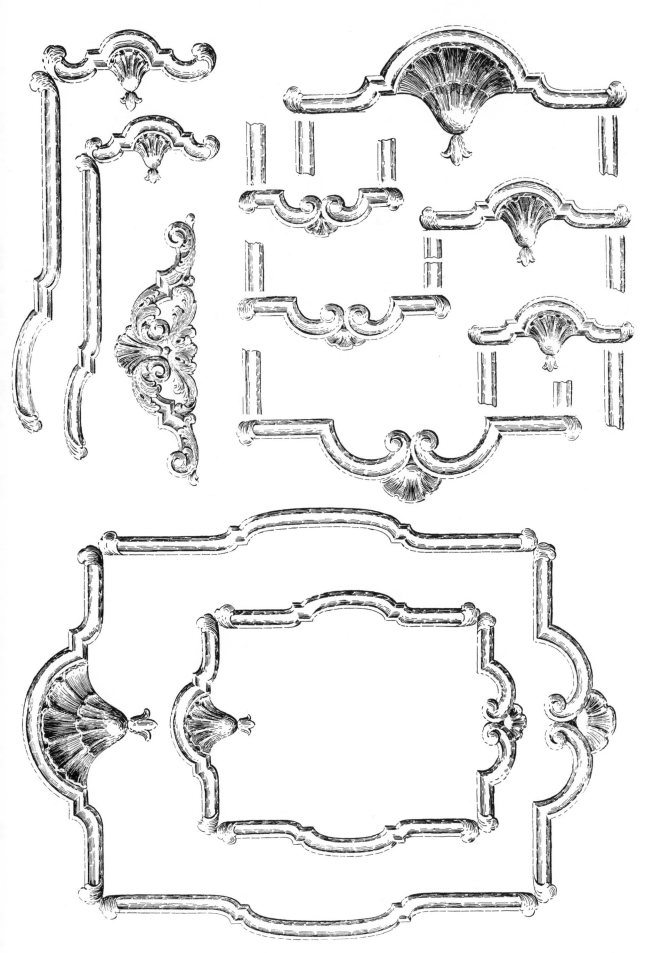

*Plate 93* Cartouches: Queen Anne and William and Mary

Plate 94   Cartouches: Georgian and Chippendale

Plate 95  Cartouches: Louis XV

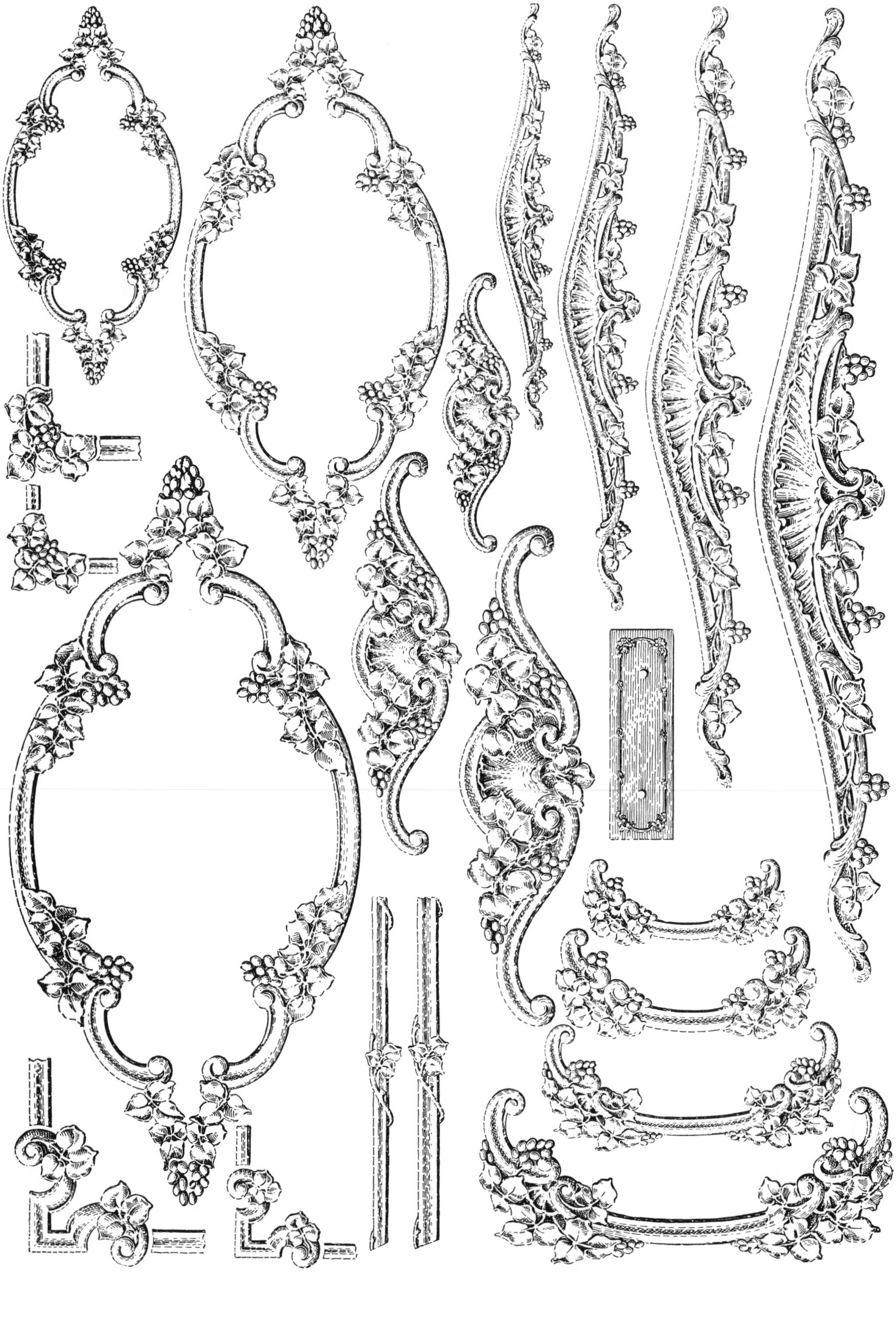

Plate 96  Cartouches: Louis XV

Plate 97   Cartouches: Louis XV

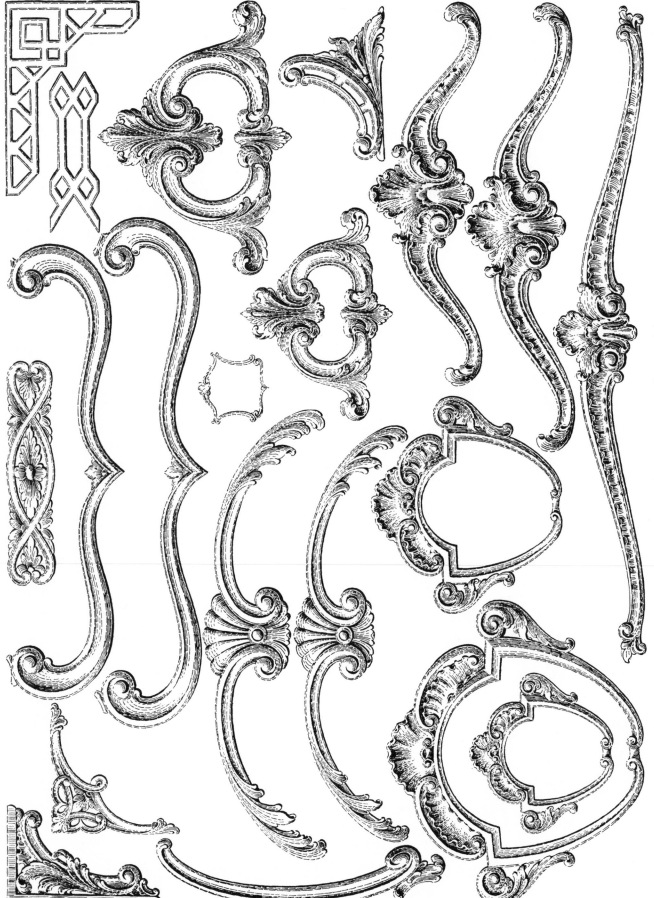

*Plate 98* Cartouches: Georgian Chippendale

*Plate 99*  Cartouches: Chippendale

Plate 100  Cartouches: Chippendale

*Plate 101*  Cartouches: French Chippendale

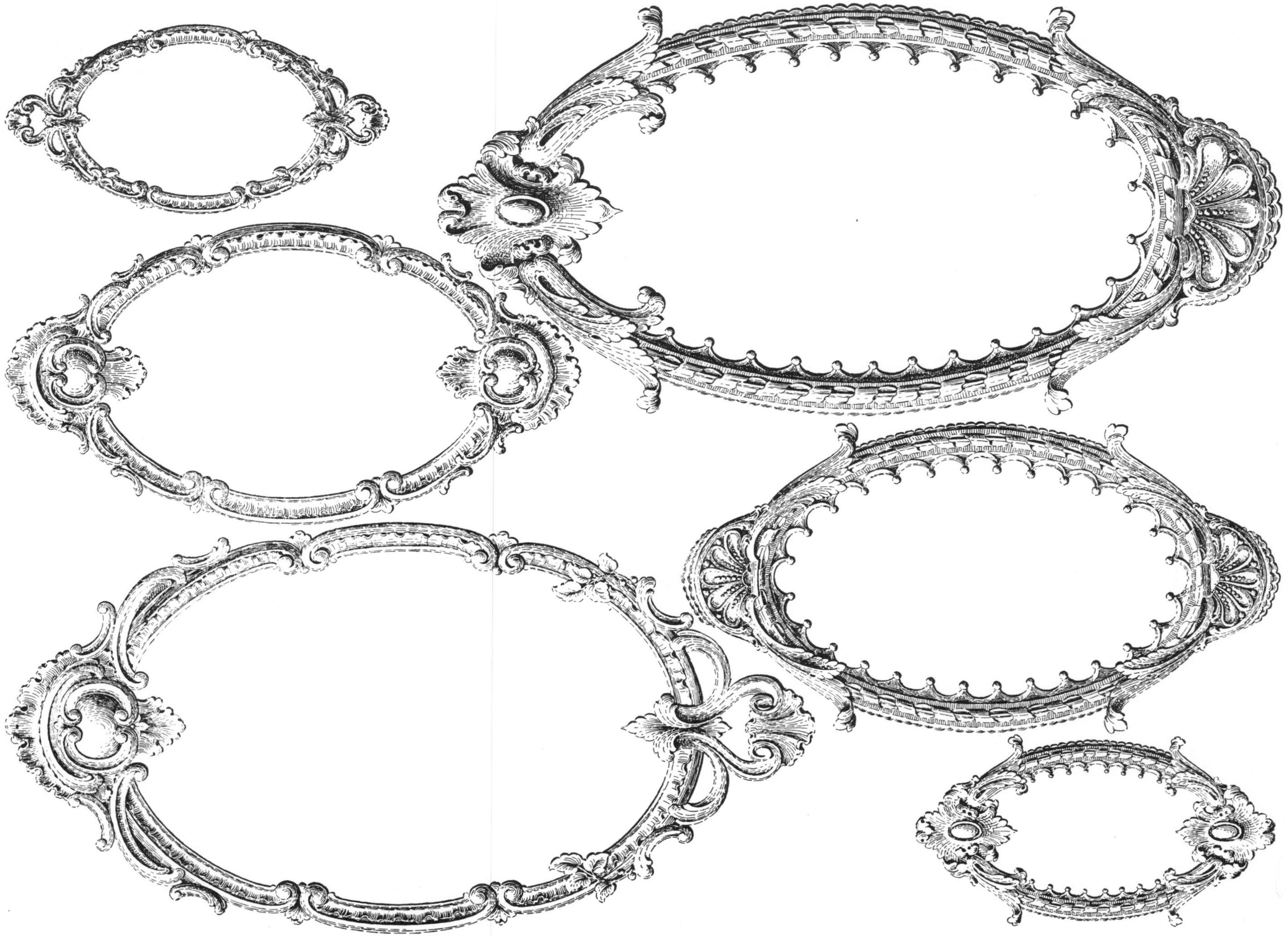

Plate 102    Cartouches: Chippendale and Louis XVI

Plate 103   Cartouches: Louis XVI

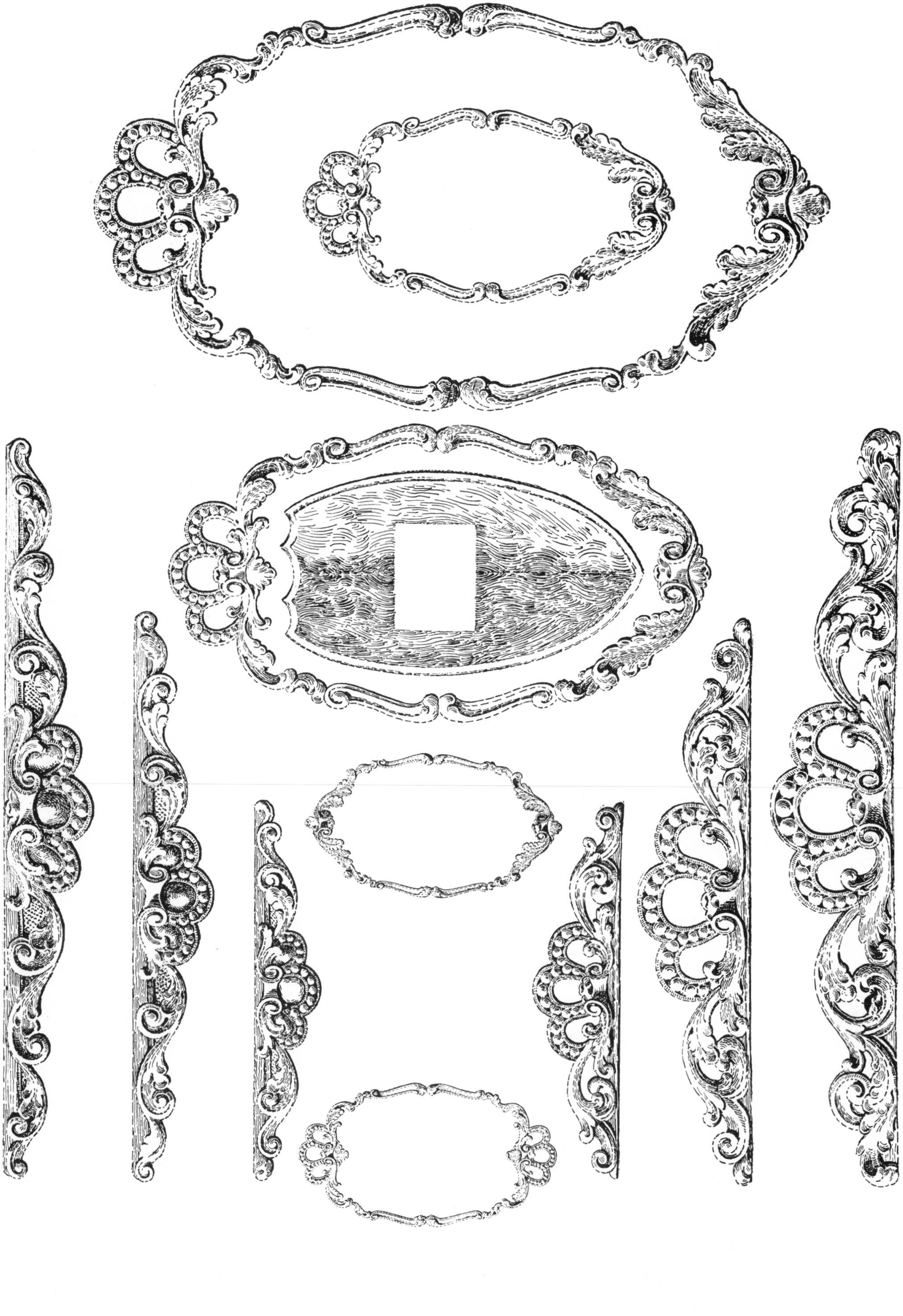

Plate 104    Cartouches: Louis XVI

Plate 105   Cartouches: Louis XVI

*Plate 106* Cartouches: Louis XVI

Plate 107 Cartouches: Louis XVI

Plate 108   Cartouches: Louis XVI

Center Line

Plate 109  Cartouches: Louis XVI

*Plate 110*  Cartouches: Louis XVI

*Plate 111* Cartouches: Louis XVI

*Plate 112*    Cartouches: Adam

*Plate 113* Cartouches: Hepplewhite

*Plate 114* Cartouches: Hepplewhite

*Plate 115* Cartouches: Hepplewhite

*Plate 116* Cartouches: Sheraton and Louis XVI (Modern Adaptation)

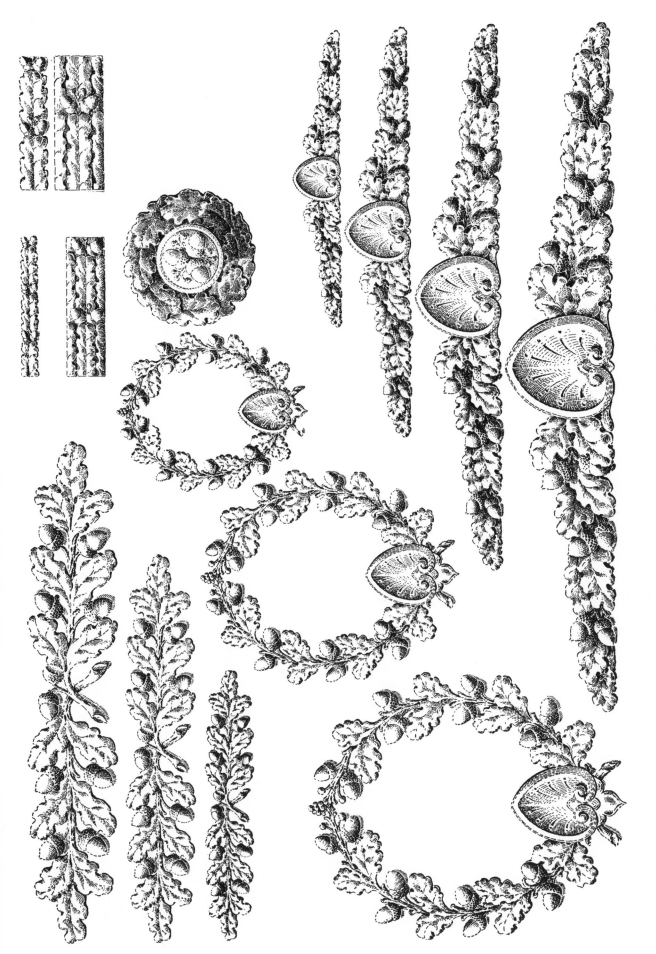

*Plate 117* Cartouches: Early American in the Duncan Phyfe Style

*Plate 118* Cartouches: Chinese

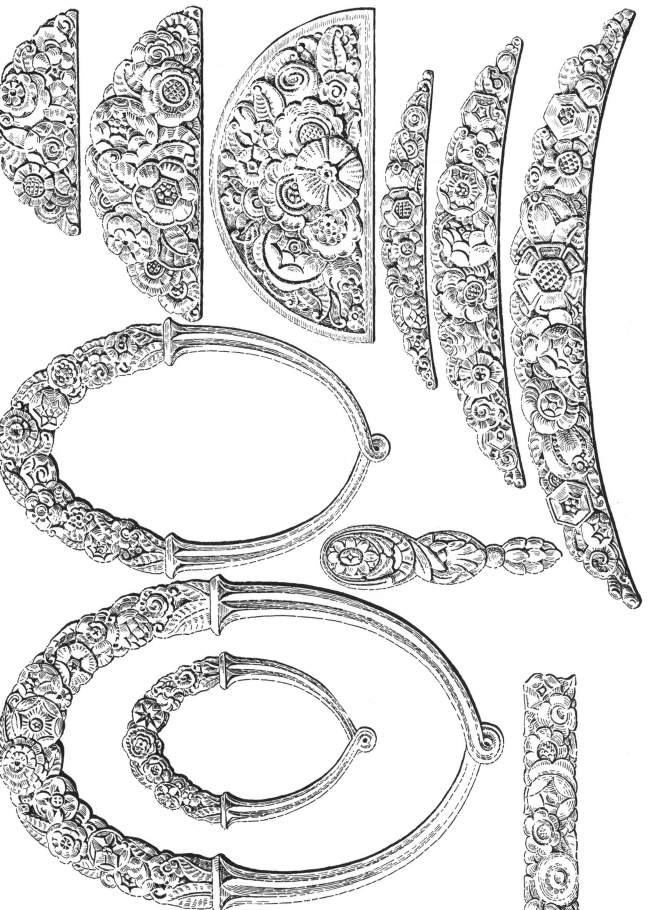

*Plate 119* Cartouches: Modern Style

*Plate 120* Cartouches: Generic Variations

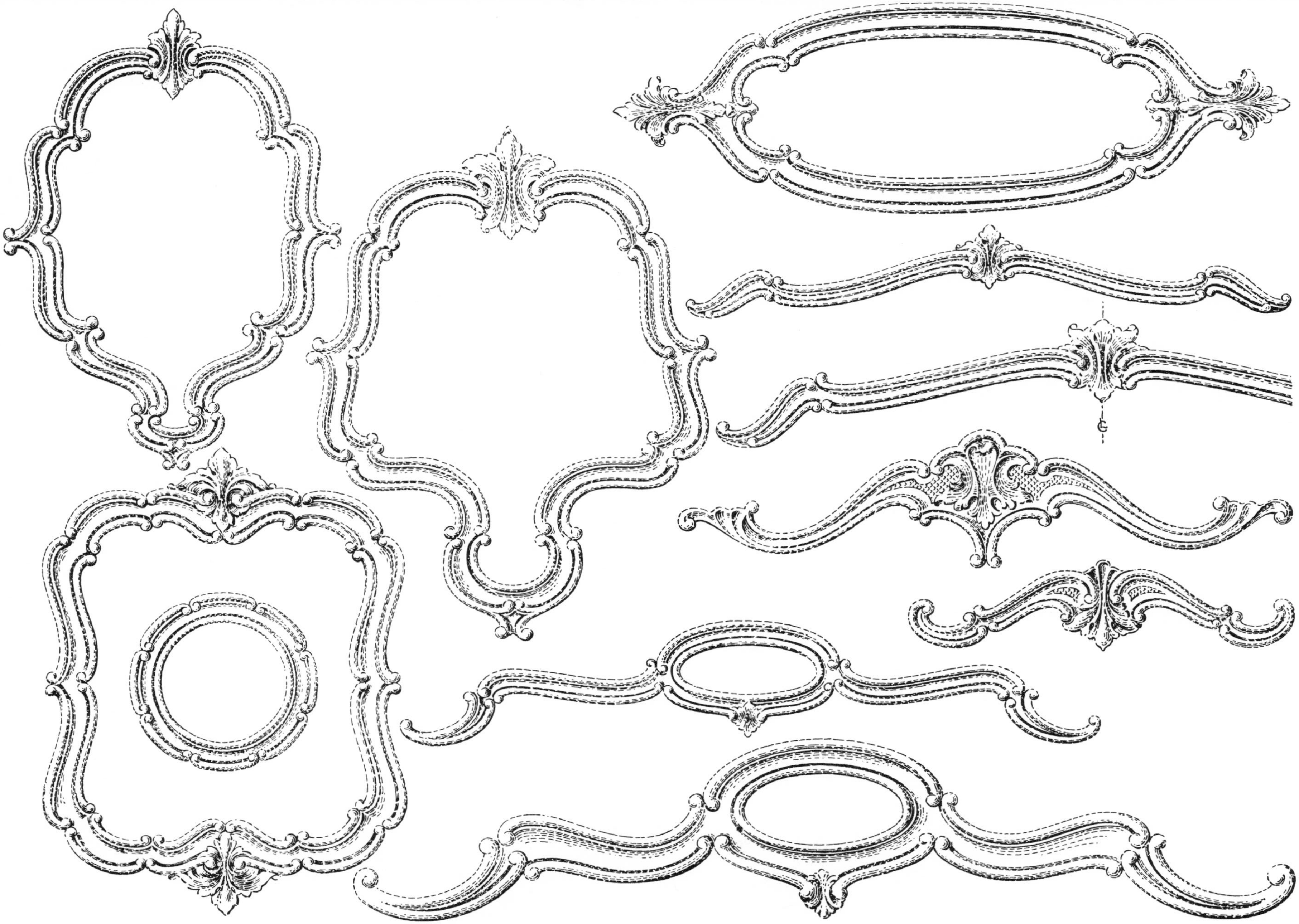

Plate 121   Cartouches: Generic Variations

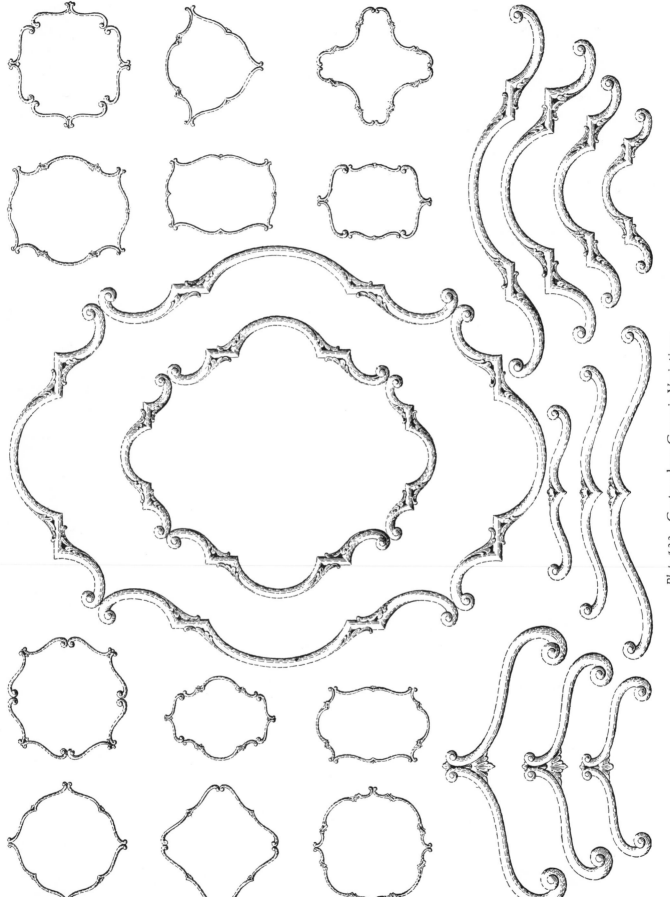

Plate 122  Cartouches: Generic Variations

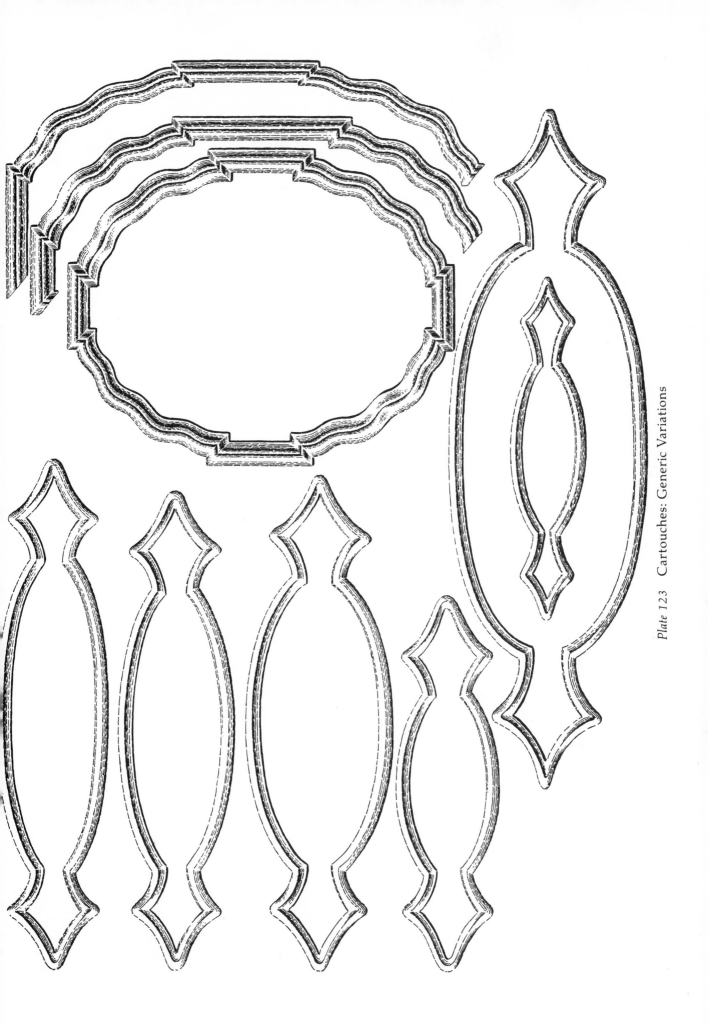

*Plate 123* Cartouches: Generic Variations

*Plate 124* Cartouches: Generic Variations

Plate 125   Cartouches: Generic Variations

8084

*Plate 126* Cartouches: Generic Variations